EVERY WORD COUNTS

The Easy Way To Win More Customers Online

ALEX WRIGHT

K
N
O
W
N

www.get-known.co.uk

DID YOU KNOW?

- There are 4.7 billion active internet users;

- Yet, less than two-thirds of small businesses have a website;

- And only 32% have a content marketing strategy;

- That is a huge missed opportunity

THIS BOOK IS FOR...

- Small professional services business owners or managers who want to improve their online brand reputation, performance and results (increase sales/profit, new customers or website visitors);

- Those who don't understand or realise the value of online content;

- Business owners or managers who don't feel confident or comfortable with writing, or don't have the necessary writing skills;

- Those who know they need to do something about their website and online presence;

- And those who don't

THIS BOOK WILL...

- Help you to step up and boost your online brand, increase sales/profit, and win new business, and drive traffic to your website;

- Help you to realise the value of online content and earn a return on your investment;

- Help you to be noticed and stand out from your competitors online;

- Help you to improve your website and other online content including blogs, newsletters and social media posts;

- Help you to improve your own writing skills and confidence

FOREWORD

BY ROBERT DILENSCHNEIDER
*Founder and Chief Executive of
The Dilenschneider Group*

This is a book for all in business but especially for small businesses.

The author, Alex Wright, is an exceptional writer, having trained his skills in the UK and abroad. He understands the value and meaning of words, and he has studied business and particularly small business for many years.

He explains why written online content is so important for small businesses; the value and power of using online content to market their business and improve their bottom line; why the website is the number one selling tool; how well-written content will get them noticed on social media; and why businesses should not overlook the power of written communication.

Of significance is that the ideas and concepts Alex presents can be used any place in the world.

His understanding of content and how it should be researched, shaped and used is exceptional.

And he understands how to use content to help the reader manage sales, excite employees, and more that will help small businesses be successful.

In a world where a website is being created every four seconds, Alex tells the reader how to develop a long-lasting attraction and delivers powerful points that will attract customers and make all audiences important to business understand the concepts needed for success.

Few ever deliver the content and ideas Alex produces.

The Dilenschneider Group is a strategic communications group serving clients around the world. Robert Dilenschneider has been called 'The Dean of Public Relations'.

MEET ALEX WRIGHT

HE IS:

- On a mission to help small businesses to improve their online content and written communication;

- A freelance copywriter and journalist specialising in finance and business;

- A former News Editor for *Insurance Times* and *Global Reinsurance*;

- A paid-up Member of ProCopywriters, the UK's largest association of commercial writers;

- A scout leader, a referee for the Under-10s Surrey Football League and a full-time 11-plus tutor to his son;

- An avid reader of travel and sports writing, and a science-fiction and horror-film fan;

- The father of two very active children, aged ten and six

HE HAS:

- More than 20 years' experience, including writing for *The Daily Mail*, *The Mail on Sunday*, *The Daily Telegraph*, *The Guardian*, *The Sunday Times*, *The Times* and *Which?* as well as business titles in the US and Australia;

- Worked in Bermuda for five years as Deputy Business Editor on the daily newspaper;

- Hosted a range of high-profile roundtables and podcasts with the business community, including Jersey Finance;

- A love of playing tennis and golf, watching Watford FC (when they're playing well) and he once ran the Bermuda marathon

CONNECT WITH ALEX ONLINE AT:

ALEXWRIGHTCOPYWRITER.COM/CONTACT

UK.LINKEDIN.COM/IN/ALEX-WRIGHT-51887438

TWITTER.COM/ALEXWCOPYWRITER

TESTIMONIALS

"I initially commissioned Alex to write the content for the homepage of a new website I was launching. He did an excellent job, getting across all the key messages clearly and concisely. Since then, he has written the homepage for my main business website, which was again of the highest standard. Because of his extensive knowledge of finance and insurance, Alex quickly gets to grips with complex ideas and presents them in an easy to understand and persuasive way. I can't recommend him highly enough."

**DR MARCUS SCHMALBACH,
FOUNDER AND CEO, RYSKEX**

"Alex Wright is a very creative and professional copywriter. He can take a glimmer of an idea and turn it into a persuasive piece of writing. He researches his subject well, being able to pull out a core message to make an engaging story that resonates with the reader. He also has a unique writing ability to connect with readers on many different subjects."

**ALISTAIR BENDYSHE-BROWN, FOUNDER/CREATIVE
DIRECTOR, SUMMER DAY MEDIA**

"A skilful researcher and versatile writer, Alex secures strong interview material and supplies punchy, well-crafted copy. I can rely on him not only to deliver to a brief, but also to approach a given topic with precision and perceptiveness."

TOM BRANTON, CONTENT DEVELOPMENT MANAGER, INSTITUTE OF DIRECTORS

"I commissioned Alex to write a short industry report and he did a sterling job. Since then, he has become my go-to man for reports, press releases, media analyses and executive summaries for conferences, covering a range of topics. He always delivers on time and to brief. What impresses me most about Alex is his highly professional can-do attitude, clear and accurate writing style and the integrity of his work."

WILL WALTER, MANAGING DIRECTOR, BRIDGEHEAD COMMUNICATIONS

"Alex is a highly capable profile writer who has been able to understand a brief from 10,000 miles away, file on time, quickly make any tweaks required, and provide the sort of copy that doesn't often require tweaks to be made at all. He has also provided story ideas which we took up, and helped to secure good photographs. He has impressed not just me but other senior staff. I recommend him without hesitation."

DAVID WALKER, EDITOR, ACUITY MAGAZINE

"My business works in the field of technology and management so Alex's experience in this field was essential. He has been helping me for the last five months, whether that is writing marketing material from scratch or reviewing my work and acting as the all-important sanity check. In both cases, Alex's knowledge and experience on crafting text for the public has shone through. In addition, he has always been able to achieve a quick turnaround in his work. He has been a pleasure to work with and I'd be more than happy to recommend him."

TONY FLEMING, OWNER,
PATHFINDER PROJECT MANAGER

"I worked with Alex Wright for four and a half years on The Royal Gazette, Bermuda's national daily newspaper. I can vouch for Alex as a tenacious, efficient and hard-working journalist, who delivered a consistently high standard of work, often under the pressure of a tight deadline. He developed a good understanding of the varied business landscape in Bermuda, ranging from the small local businesses to the multibillion-dollar global insurers, and built a broad network of contacts here across the full spectrum."

JONATHAN KENT, ASSISTANT EDITOR,
THE ROYAL GAZETTE

"I have known Alex Wright for a number of years, having met him in Bermuda when I was posted there by Schroders as managing director of their subsidiary there, Schroders (Bermuda) Limited. I have always liked his style, the presentational aspects and his commentary. He has an impressive knowledge of financial markets in general, coupled with a good background in the supportive economics. We also became friends over time and I value his friendship."

DAVID BURNS, NON-EXECUTIVE MEMBER OF THE BOARD OF TREA SA, ON THE ADVISORY BOARD OF THE TREA DIRECT LENDING FUND AND BLACK TORO CAPITAL, ADVISOR TO PAKENHAM PARTNERS LIMITED

"Alex is simply the most versatile journalist I have worked with in my 20-year career. It's not just his ability to address several topics as a specialist. Added to that is his ability to write in different styles – entertaining newspaper prose one day and then the following day a prescriptive client advertorial, both with equal competence and verve. A really good guy, always with an interesting observation that cuts through any nonsense."

DAVID BANKS, POLITICAL RESEARCHER AND DIRECTOR OF IMAGINEXIT AND FORMER INSURANCE MAGAZINE EDITOR

CONTENTS

1

HOW THIS BOOK
WILL HELP YOU

WHO I AM

Welcome to my book. My name is Alex Wright and I am a Freelance Copywriter and Journalist with more than 20 years' experience of writing online content. After successfully completing my diploma in newspaper journalism, I started out on local papers before shifting for the nationals, including *The Daily Telegraph* and *The Sunday Times*.

Then I had the fortune to land a job as Deputy Business Editor on Bermuda's daily paper. There I honed my craft, engaging with and writing about business people from a cross-section of different industries.

On my return to the UK, I worked as News Editor for a range of specialist trade magazines covering the financial services sector before building up enough contacts to branch out on my own. Soon after, I took a copywriting course to add another string to my bow, since when I have been helping businesses with their written communication strategies, writing their websites, blogs and newsletters, as well as offering advice on social media posts, among other online content.

WHY I WROTE THIS BOOK

The guiding principle I have abided by throughout my career has been to help others to tell their story. Allied to this is my passion for helping small professional services businesses with producing their online content. The buzz and feeling of pride I get from helping businesses achieve success with their online content is immense.

"

Many business owners
view having a website
as a necessary chore
and don't see the value
of words.

"

Having worked with many different businesses across multiple sectors, I have identified a big problem that all have in common.

Many business owners view having a website as a necessary chore and don't see the value of words. Because of this, they are missing a prime opportunity to sell themselves.

Often they have a poor online presence, whether that is an underperforming website or a lack of engagement on social media – or they don't have any at all. Worse still, their website is badly structured or written, or they are adopting the wrong strategy altogether, ultimately doing more harm than good to their brand.

The Covid-19 pandemic has exacerbated this issue, with many businesses realising what they have is insufficient and hastily trying to find a quick fix, largely because their peers have told them that they need to, or they are worried about what their competitors were doing. What they are doing, however, is in effect simply wasting their precious time, energy and money.

HOW YOU WILL BENEFIT

If you are the owner or manager of a small professional services business, this book is for you. It will help you to understand why getting online content right is key to your success in an increasingly competitive world, where you need to stand out from your rivals.

I will provide you with key tips and advice, and equip you with tried and tested tools to help you improve your online content, enabling you to enhance your brand image, customer base and sales/profit. I will also show you how to get noticed online and drive more traffic to your website.

Like all my writing, this book is written in clear, simple and jargon-free language that anyone new to the subject can understand, and is easily accessible. You don't need any prior experience of writing for online either – this book will give you all the basic skills required to structure and write engaging content that your target audience will want to read.

HOW TO USE THIS BOOK

This book is designed either to be read from cover to cover or for dipping into as and when you need to. However, if you are unfamiliar with writing for online, I recommend starting from the beginning, because that is where the most relevant and timely chapters are.

If you need any more information or support in a particular area covered in this book, for example, writing website content, blogs or for social media, get in touch at **alexwrightcopywriter.com**. Believe me, I have seen many businesses like yours, struggling to get the most from their online content and scratching their heads because they don't know why it isn't working for them. And I'd love to hear from you.

Your website and online content are vital to the success of your business, so don't neglect them.

Without further ado, let's begin.

SUMMARY

✓ You will benefit from the advice and insight of an online content expert who has been there and done it all;

✓ I want to help small business owners and managers like you to improve your online content – and bottom line;

✓ I will help you to understand the critical importance of getting your online content right;

✓ This book is written in a clear, simple and jargon-free way so it is easy for everyone to understand;

✓ It is designed to be read as a whole or chapter by chapter

2

WHY YOU NEED TO IMPROVE YOUR ONLINE PRESENCE

THE IMPORTANCE OF AN ONLINE PRESENCE

Quite simply, everyone is online now. If you are not there, you are missing out, potentially on many lucrative new deals.

Most consumers go online first to do their research on a company, or product or service before deciding what to do. One survey reported that 92% of those who buy property searched online as part of the process.

You need to be first in the queue when people embark on their online buying journey. My homepage at **alexwrightcopywriter.com** is a good example of how to set out clearly what your business does in a way that is easy for the customer to understand.

You also need to be online just to stay in touch with your existing customers and suppliers, so they know you are still there. That has been particularly important during the pandemic, with many companies having to close their stores and the uncertainty around their ability to trade.

Before you go any further, let's see how effective your online presence is by taking this free and simple five-step test, which will tell you what you need to focus on or do next: **alexwrightcopywriter.com/website-and-online-content-review/**

WHAT 'CLICK-THROUGH' AND 'BOUNCE RATES' MEAN

You may have heard of the terms click-through and bounce rate and wondered what on earth they mean. They are both vital to helping you improve your website content.

Your bounce rate tells you what percentage of visitors to your website landed on one of your pages but left without visiting any others. Therefore, the higher the bounce rate, the fewer visitors who are engaging with your website; the lower, the more are engaging and visiting other pages.

The optimal bounce is between 26-40%; 56% to 70% is average; above 70% is cause for concern. A 100% bounce rate would mean that no one is engaging with your website at all and you need to take immediate action.

If you take out an advert, your click-through rate (or CTR) tells you how often people who see that advert end up clicking on it. The opposite of the bounce rate is true of your CTR: the higher it is the better, because it means more people are interested in your advert.

You can work out both your bounce and click-through rates using analytics programs such as Google Analytics. I run a monthly report to look at these figures in more detail and see what pages or adverts are doing well and which need improving.

"

_____

Make sure you have

answered the five Ws:

what, where, who, when

and why, as well as how.

_____

"

HOW TO WRITE FOR ONLINE

First, think about the purpose of your piece. Is it driving sales or traffic to your website, or generating interest in your brand?

Online pieces tend to be shorter than in print because, on average, people spend less time reading a screen. Set yourself a length, by way of a word limit that isn't too long, but is enough to capture the main points you want to make without your audience switching off.

The length of the piece will vary depending on the subject and the depth you want to go into. If, for example, you are writing a blog post, I would recommend writing between 300 and 750 words, which makes it easier to find on search engines.

As with any piece, start with a strong introduction with the most interesting angle(s) for your reader, presented in an opening paragraph of no more than three sentences. Within that introduction, make sure you have answered the five Ws: what, where, who, when and why, as well as how. For example: Lady Godiva (who) rode (what) naked (how) through the streets of Coventry (where) yesterday (when) in a bid to cut taxes (why).

The main types of introduction are:

- Factual/topical (eg Local law firm creates 10 jobs under ambitious expansion plans);

- Historical (eg A family-run accountancy firm is offering free consultations to the first 20 customers that sign up, to mark 20 years in business);

- Anecdotal/short story/scene setter (eg Imagine you didn't have to sweat over filing your tax return on time like you do every year. That dream can become a reality thanks to Government's new making tax digital scheme);

- Surprise/juxtaposition (eg While many companies have suffered a decline in business, one local architectural firm is bucking the trend, with enquiries up 500% this month);

- Question (eg Did you know that fewer than two thirds of small businesses have a website?)

Expand upon each of those key points in the middle of your article as you build your narrative using quotes where possible to reinforce each argument. Add background later where needed. Once you have outlined your main points, you need to make sure they all link together in a coherent and logical manner from one to the next.

Present your key arguments first and your counterarguments afterwards, using quotes, where possible, to back them up and add information. After you have made a point, move onto the next one.

Put any additional information or side story that doesn't fit within the flow of the narrative in a box. Wrap it all up with a summary of your main points.

The main types of conclusion are:

- Summarising what you have said (eg In summary, investing in a good copywriter was the best thing I ever did);

- Reflecting on the key issue (eg The wide-ranging implications of the latest tax changes are there for all to see);

- Quote (eg 'Never has there been a better opportunity to invest in trust funds');

- Looking to the future (eg If sales continue in this fashion, the company will have a bright future ahead)

CASE STUDY

A great example of producing quality online content is Hargreaves Lansdown. The investment service headquartered in Bristol has built itself from a relatively small base to become one of the most respected names in the industry.

Part of its success has been down to its comprehensive online content strategy, providing customers with timely and relevant information through their preferred medium, whether that is visiting the website or through its email newsletter or social media.

By keeping in regular contact with its customers, the firm stays in the front of their minds. This way, it can also capture more information about its customers and target them with the appropriate content.

SUMMARY

✓ You need to be at the front of the queue when customers go online to search for your product or service;

✓ You want to maintain a low bounce rate, which means visitors are engaging more with your website;

✓ Keep online content short and to the point;

✓ Make sure you cover the five Ws (and an H) in your introduction;

✓ Expand on each of your key points in the middle before rounding off your piece with a strong conclusion

3

WHY YOU NEED
ONLINE CONTENT

WHY ONLINE CONTENT IS SO IMPORTANT

Anyone who is serious about business is online now, both your clients and competitors. The potential to reach a wider audience and, thus, win more business has never been greater.

Therefore, you want to present your business and website in the best possible light. Fail to do so and you are just throwing money away in lost sales and business, metaphorically speaking.

Having the right online presence with well-written content is key to all this. Whether it is persuading shoppers to visit your website with a free offer or selling your product or service in a newsletter, it all hinges on how you get your message across.

HOW ONLINE CONTENT IS KEY TO YOUR SUCCESS

Think of your website as a virtual shop front, where you have an opportunity to sell to anyone that visits it. Just as you would in a bricks and mortar high street shop, you need to present the opportunity in the best possible fashion to entice people in.

Once they are in, it is your prime opportunity to sell to them. You do that by using the right words that customers want or need to hear, so that they are likely to spend money with you and return to spend more.

On the other hand, if your display is poorly presented, with sloppy spelling, grammar and punctuation, people are unlikely to want to visit. Remember that you work in professional services: therefore your customer will expect only the highest standards.

"

Think of your website
as a virtual shop front,
where you have an
opportunity to sell to
anyone that visits it.

"

As an absolute basic, having an online presence during the pandemic has enabled many businesses that operate stores to continue trading. But with so many of your competitors online, to make you stand out it is essential that you ensure your content is of the highest quality.

HOW YOU WILL BENEFIT FROM WORKING WITH A PROFESSIONAL COPYWRITER

While this book will teach you some invaluable tips and insight on how to improve your online content that you won't get anywhere else, it is also aimed as an introduction to the subject. Don't expect to become a writing expert overnight, but if you begin to feel more confident about your writing ability, then you are making good progress.

If you feel that you need further support, however, it is worth investing in a professional copywriter such as me to help you, whether it is devising your written communication strategy, writing a website and blogs for you, or just to get some advice on social media posts [get in touch at **alexwrightcopywriter.com/contact**]. In return, you can expect to receive a highly professional and quality service, as well as reaping the rewards of increased sales/profit, new clients or website traffic, depending on your long-term goal.

Don't just take my word for it either. See my testimonials section at the beginning of this book to read what some of my clients have to say about the service they received.

CASE STUDY

I was approached by a family-run high street tax advice firm to help set up its website. The business had been reasonably successful within its town but it wanted to expand its customer base across the county.

After looking at how we could attract more customers through the use of online, we set up a simple website with home, services and contact pages. Within three months, the site brought in 50 new enquiries, 10 of which were converted into sales.

That is the difference between having an online presence and having none. If the business wasn't online it wouldn't have been found by these customers searching for tax advice in the first place.

SUMMARY

✓ Everyone is online so the potential to reach a larger audience is huge;

✓ If you fail to make the most of your online presence, you are just throwing money away;

✓ Your website is like a virtual shop front used to entice customers in;

✓ Yours is a professional business and your online content should reflect that;

✓ Invest in a professional copywriter to help you get the best results

4

HOW TO REACH YOUR TARGET AUDIENCE

HOW TO DETERMINE WHAT YOUR TARGET AUDIENCE REALLY WANTS

As a business owner or manager, you will have in mind a target audience who you want to sell your product or service to. Once you have established who that target market is, you need to decide what it is they are looking for or are going to be most interested in.

However, while you may think you know what they want, because you have been doing things a certain way, often you can overlook what is really important to them. Instead, you need to take a step back and look at the bigger picture or bring in a professional copywriter like me to look at what they really want [get in touch at **alexwrightcopywriter.com/contact**].

If you are doing this yourself, you need to carry out extensive market research to identify trends that drive buying behaviour, needs and desires. Use analytics programs such as Google Analytics to see the most commonly searched-for terms and determine those which you can use to create a niche for yourself. You should also look at what your competitors are doing, how successful they are and whether you can use, adapt or expand on some of their methods.

If you scored lowly in my five-step test, this chapter will help you to improve your audience engagement.

HOW TO GET YOUR MESSAGE ACROSS SIMPLY AND CLEARLY

When you are writing, always think about what your reader wants. I have seen too many businesses that make the mistake of focusing on themselves rather than the customer.

Use as few words as necessary to make your point.

You need to concentrate on the 'you' and why your product or service is important for the customer and what they will derive from it. This boils down to the key features and benefits of what you are selling, such as ease of use or helping people to save money.

Think about how they are likely to use the product or service, what they want to achieve from it and the value they will get from it. Then explain in the simplest terms how they will benefit, eg it will 'help you to get the job done more easily' or 'save you lots of money'.

Think:

- Who is visiting my website?

- What are they looking for?

- How will they get there?

- How can I give them the most relevant information as easily as possible?

- What is the easiest way for them to get in touch?

Another common error that I see is businesses thinking they need to use as many words as possible to get their message across. In fact, the opposite is true: your audience will switch off if you give them too much information, so use as few words as necessary to make your point.

HOW TO MEASURE YOUR RESULTS

The best way to determine the success of your approach is ultimately in the sales you make. It's easier to measure if you have changed your key messaging, but you can also see what is working best, and why, by using analytics programs on the most visited pages of your website and those your customer spends the most time on.

Finding out where most of your traffic is coming from is also invaluable, so that you can target the right communication channels, whether it is from search engines, email newsletters or social media. Again, you can do this through analytics programs by setting the metrics to help you find exactly what you are looking for.

You should also seek feedback from your customers to see if they found what they were looking for and how easily they found it, as well as how you can improve the process for them. By using all of this information in conjunction, you can improve your online content to best meet your customers' needs.

CASE STUDY

A local construction firm was trying to sell new luxury homes in a village for retirees to downsize into. Despite a considerable marketing effort and spend, sales were slow.

Investigation revealed that buyers were primarily interested in having a large enough space for their dining room tables so their families could gather at Christmas. After changing the focus of its product to make the key feature 'enough space to have the whole family for Christmas dinner', sales took off.

By taking a step back and considering the bigger picture, the firm was able to understand what its target market was really looking for. By changing its key message to reflect that, it was able to capture far more sales than if it had stuck with its initial approach.

SUMMARY

✓ Determine what your target audience wants;

✓ Consider investing in a professional copywriter such as me to help you identify what people are looking for;

✓ Focus on the 'you' and why your product or service is important to the customer;

✓ Explain the key benefits in the simplest terms;

✓ Use analytics programs to see which pages your customers are looking at most and how they are getting there

5

THE IMPORTANCE OF A COMPELLING HEADLINE

WHY HEADLINES ARE SO IMPORTANT

Your headline is the most important part of your online content, whether it is for a blog on your website or in your email newsletter. The headline will often determine whether your audience will want to read the rest of your piece.

"

The difference between a powerful and a poorly written headline can be the difference between a sale and no sale.

"

A strong and interesting headline will inspire your customer to continue reading. A weak and uninspiring headline will prompt them to stop and go somewhere else.

The headline sums up your key message: if it is the only thing people read, they will at least know the main point you want to get across. After discovering that five times more people read the headline than the article, advertising guru David Ogilvy described headlines as 'as close to a magic bullet as you're going to get'.

WHY YOU NEED AN EYE-GRABBING HEADLINE

All the headlines used online scream for your attention. To make yours stand out, you need a headline that grabs readers' attention from the first word and makes them want to read on.

Therefore, you need to come up with a headline that really jumps out from the page and makes your reader sit up and take notice. The difference between a powerful and a poorly written headline can be the difference between a sale and no sale.

For example, consider the headline: 'Health company launches new product'; that is of limited interest to the reader. Now consider: 'New health kick gets you up off the sofa'. The focus on the benefit makes it far more appealing.

HOW TO WRITE A COMPELLING HEADLINE

As well as making an instant impression, you need to give your audience the essence of what your piece is about. So think about how best to sum it all up in no more than five to ten words. You can always add a 20- to 25-word sub-heading underneath, expanding upon the main point you have made.

Keep your headline simple yet informative. Avoid alliteration, puns, funny one-liners or trying to be too clever. My blog page at **alexwrightcopywriter.com/ blog** has some good examples of how to write headlines that explain exactly what the posts are about.

Also think about using intrigue to make the reader want to find out what happens next. If you are unsure how your customer will likely react, try it out on your colleagues or peers to see what they think.

Here are the three main types of headlines you should aim to use:

1. New angle

Thanks to the advent of social media, there is no such thing as an exclusive story. But you can always offer a new insight into, or angle on, an old story. A view counter to the consensus will often be more interesting to your audience; it challenges convention and offers something different.

With so many negative stories out there, this is your chance to find something positive and sell it. So, look at what has been done before and see how you can improve upon it or interpret it in a different way. But make sure that your argument stands up, backed up with accurate and relevant facts, figures, quotes and anecdotal evidence.

2. Self-help

Self-help pieces tell readers how to improve themselves, through wealth, health, happiness, wisdom or other means. These pieces often come in the form of lists or bullet points, such as 'how to' guides and Top 5s or 10s.

When you write your headline, you need to make sure that it accurately reflects the main narrative and isn't just an unjustifiable claim intended to lure more readers. Think hard about what readers would be most interested in knowing about and how you can appeal to them.

3. Human interest

People are nosy by nature and want to know about other people's lives. We all do. That's why social media is so popular.

The best way to feed curiosity is to write a compelling headline about an interesting person other people will be curious about and therefore can't resist reading about. That could be a rags-to-riches tale, a story about overcoming disaster or illness, or one of abject failure.

CASE STUDY

Amazon is a classic example of how to use a headline to sell your product. Often the best headlines are the ones that describe simply what the product or service is and what it does.

The basic formula is '[Product/Service] is a [Description] that helps you [Action]'. For example: 'Amazon Dash Button is a wi-fi connected device that reorders your favourite product with the press of a button'.

This clearly sets out the key features and benefits this product offers the customer. It also makes it easier to find on search engines when the customer is looking for that particular term.

SUMMARY

✓ Headlines are the most important part of your online content;

✓ Your audience is much more likely to read and take in a strong and interesting headline;

✓ A powerful headline can be the difference between a sale and no sale;

✓ Use a headline to sum up your piece in no more than five to ten words;

✓ Keep your headline simple but, where possible, use intrigue to make the reader want to find out more

6

GETTING YOUR STRUCTURE AND TONE RIGHT

WHY STRUCTURE IS SO IMPORTANT

The second most important part of online content is having a solid structure in place. Like a powerful headline, it determines how easy it is for your audience to read and understand the piece.

Think of your structure like building a house. You need to have the right parts in place in the right order to ensure that the foundation is strong and it all fits together properly.

A weak structure means your house is more likely to fall apart. In the same way, your writing will be hard for readers to follow and they will ultimately abandon it. Presented well, your words can show off the best features of your construction and draw in a wider audience.

If you scored poorly in my five-step test, this chapter will provide you with the building blocks for a solid foundation for your website and online content.

HOW TO STRUCTURE YOUR CONTENT

Before you start, think carefully about the best way to present your writing so that it is easy to follow, concise and engaging. Plan what you are going to write about, with a central theme backed up by supporting arguments arranged in a clear and logical order that flows.

As you write each sentence, think carefully about the point you want to make and how you can do it in as few words as possible. Assume that your reader knows nothing about the subject. If you can't understand what you have written, they are unlikely to either. Read some of my blogs at **alexwrightcopywriter.com/blog** for good examples of how to structure your content so that it is easy to read.

"

Write in short sentences
(no more than 20 words)
to give your statements
more purpose.

"

Think:

- What are the main points you want to get across?

- What order of importance will you put them in?

- How will you connect each point in a logical order so that your piece flows?

- How will you conclude the piece?

Write in short sentences (no more than 20 words) to give your statements more purpose. Use two- or three-sentence paragraphs for each point you want to make. The first sentence or two should make the point (the cause) and the others should support that point (the effect).

Write in the same way as you would speak and don't use complicated words that people are unlikely to understand. Don't get hung up with cramming in as many key words as possible to improve your search engine ranking: rather use original similes and metaphors to paint a picture. Also, remember that full stops are free: the more you can use to break up your sentences, the better.

Use sub-headings and bullet points regularly to emphasise each key point you want to make. Images, infographics and pull quotes also help to break up the text, making it easier for your audience to digest. You should use at least three links per page to direct them to specific pages on your website or another reliable source for more information or to sell to them.

HOW TO DECIDE ON A STYLE AND TONE

Decide on a style and stick to it for consistency's sake. Your tone should be clear, simple and accessible, yet you should come across as an authority on the subject who knows about the subject matter inside and out.

Your style and tone should also reflect your own brand values, vision and key messaging. That way your customer will know what to expect from you and therefore trust that you will deliver on it.

Adopt an active voice in the present tense that is direct and personal. Bring your piece to life with crisp and meaningful verbs, placing the subject first (eg 'Keen investors snapped up the shares', rather than 'The shares were snapped up by keen investors'). If you are covering a traditionally dry topic, such as finance or accountancy, where possible humanise it by using real-life examples of people and their experiences.

HOW TO REVIEW AND EDIT

Once you have written your piece, go back and review it thoroughly. Read it through first for spelling, grammar and punctuation, using a spell check, and also make sure you fact-check everything. Make sure you can back up everything you write.

Then read it again, ideally 24 hours later, to make sure it reads well and makes sense, getting all your key points across as concisely and easily to understand as possible.

Think:

- Is it directed at your target audience?

- What will they get out of it?

- Are your key points in the right order?

- Is it clear and does it flow?

- Are the arguments and counter-arguments balanced?

- Is there any repetition?

- Does it have enough quotes?

- Are the grammar, spelling and punctuation correct?

- Does it feel the right length?

- What is missing?

I find that it helps to print your piece out and read it out loud to yourself to hear how it sounds. Ask one of your colleagues or peers to read it afterwards as they may highlight any mistakes that you have missed or recommend ways to improve it.

MINDING YOUR Ps AND Qs

Good use of grammar, spelling and punctuation is the foundation of a well-constructed piece. To achieve this, you need to focus on getting the basics right and avoid being too clever or getting bogged down in the detail.

Think about the easiest way you can write a sentence to make your point. Leave out words that don't add any detail to your piece.

Starting with the grammar: avoid turning nouns into verbs, which just ends up sounding like boring corporate speak. The words 'access', 'resource' and 'impact' are prime examples.

Remember that singular nouns (eg Government, politics and the United States of America) use the singular verb 'is' and collective nouns (eg companies, families and employees) use the plural verb 'are'. For your purposes, the simple rule of thumb is that 'is' is used as the verb for what a business does.

Don't use the word 'whom': it is only correct in certain contexts. Use 'who' instead. Likewise, avoid using the word 'as': as one of my editors at *The Sunday*

Times said to me, it is lazy grammar used to join two statements together.

The word 'think' in reported speech is another redundant word. After all, everyone 'thinks' before they say something. Similarly, 'literally' adds nothing new to a sentence, other than an extra word.

Other words that are often misused are fewer and less. Fewer is used where items can be counted, such as oranges. Less is used where an item can't be counted, such as orange juice.

As far as punctuation is concerned, don't use an adjective where you don't have to: over-description is lost on your audience. Instead, use a strong metaphor or simile to make your point.

Use a full stop after each point you have made. If you are unsure about whether to use a semi-colon, don't.

Also, use commas sparingly – only for clauses in the middle of a sentence – and where possible break down the sentence with full stops after each point. A comma used in the wrong place can change the whole meaning of a sentence.

Where the word 'however' is used at the start of a sentence, add a comma after it. However, if it is used in the middle, put commas either side of it.

Use apostrophes to shorten your sentence. As a rule of thumb, it is 's when you are writing in the singular possessive and s' if it is plural (eg my cat's friendly; her six cats' shrieks drive me crazy). Or it is used to signify where a letter or word is missing, often combining two words (eg wouldn't, you've etc).

Only use quote marks for direct speech. Finish every quote with a quotation mark. Everyone has different house styles, but most people use double quote marks in the main piece and single quotes in the headline and/ or sub-heading. Whichever style you use, be consistent.

Wherever possible, use an active voice in the present tense to add power to your sentence, but in some cases, where it's more appropriate, you may have to use the passive. People are much more interested in the here and now.

Don't get hung up on split infinitives either – where a word is inserted between the word 'to' and the verb – but try to avoid them if you can. Also, it is fine to finish a sentence with a preposition – a word or phrase which connects a noun or pronoun with a verb or adjective. Likewise, there is no rule to say you can't start a sentence with the word 'because'.

Lastly, pay careful attention to spell checks, particularly if you are using an American English version. They are not always right. Always go back and edit your piece and also ask a qualified person such as an editor to review it afterwards.

Above all, don't overthink it; just write. It is better to have a story that flows well before bringing in the grammar police.

CASE STUDY

A double-glazing firm commissioned me to write a landing page to promote its core product to homeowners. The page needed to cover the reasons for using the product and why readers should choose this particular firm.

I started with a story before convincing the customer why it was essential and finished by telling them how they could get hold of it. I applied the AIDA principle of selling: get your audience's **A**ttention, pique their **I**nterest in the product, make them **D**esire it and get them to take **A**ction by buying it.

The structure was as follows:

Headline: A simple home improvement that pays for itself

Introduction: Story of a retired couple who used a cowboy firm to install their windows and lived to regret it

Middle: Explain that they had the right idea in wanting to improve their home with double-glazing and the financial benefit they could obtain in energy savings and the resale value of their house, using facts and figures to back it up

Outline the other key benefits including appearance and soundproofing

Expand on why you need to watch out for cowboys and how to pick a reputable firm

Detail how the firm ticks all the boxes with its key values, supported by strong customer reviews

Explain the process of what happens when the customer contacts the firm

Conclusion: Offer a 10% discount to customers who sign up today for a quote

SUMMARY

✓ The structure is what holds your piece together;

✓ Plan carefully beforehand how all the different elements of your piece are going to fit together;

✓ Write in short, easy to understand sentences;

✓ Decide on a style and tone – and stick to it;

✓ Once you have written your piece, review it thoroughly

7

WHY WRITING FOR DIFFERENT ONLINE FORMATS IS SO IMPORTANT

The different kinds of medium for online content are almost endless. Aside from your website and social media, there are blogs, newsletters and tip sheets, press releases, articles, white papers and company reports, to name but a few.

"

Because each format has
its own purpose, is meant
for different audiences,
and is consumed in
different ways, it is
essential to provide a
range of online content.

"

Because each format has its own purpose, is meant for different audiences, and is consumed in different ways, it is essential to provide a range of online content. A reader who visits your website to look at a product or service may not necessarily want to receive email newsletters and vice versa.

The more bases you can cover, the more likely you are to appeal to a wider audience, provided your content is targeted and relevant. Of course, much of it can also be repackaged and used again in a different format (eg blogs can be used on your website and feature in your weekly newsletter as well).

HOW TO BE CONSISTENT IN YOUR KEY MESSAGING

Although each format varies slightly in terms of style and structure (eg white papers are longer and more detailed than blog posts), the same fundamental rules apply when writing content. You should use a strong headline and introduction, keep your sentences short and sharp, and make your narrative flow from point to point.

Blogs are written in a more conversational style, while press releases, company reports and white papers are more formal. But don't forget to maintain a tone of voice that reflects the key values and mission statement of your business.

Also, be consistent: if you say one thing on one platform, don't contradict it on another. If you do, it will be quickly seized upon and you will lose face in the eyes of the customer.

I'm not going to go into much more detail here as there are so many different types of medium available. But if you're looking for more information about how to write in different formats, get in touch at **alexwrightcopywriter.com/ contact** or visit my blog at **alexwrightcopywriter.com/ blog**. I'll be happy to help.

CUTTING THROUGH THE NOISE

Blogs are essentially a tool to provide your target audience with useful information in an easy-to-read narrative format. They should add value by telling your readers something they don't already know or could benefit from.

Here are my five simple steps for writing a blog:

1. Come up with an original idea

With millions of blogs produced every day, you need to come up with one that stands out from the rest. It should also be relevant to your target audience (eg if your core market is weddings, you should write a guide on how to find the best wedding dress or make the best wedding cake).

Focus on the key challenges your clients face and potential solutions. Also, ask your customers for feedback on what they would like to know about and look at what your competitors are doing to see how you can build upon that.

2. Decide on a snappy headline and introduction

Once you have settled on an idea, come up with a headline that will grab your audience's attention. It needs to be short and clear, and contain the key words and phrases that they are likely searching for.

Remember to limit your introduction to a paragraph of three sentences covering all the key points you want to address as well as the 5Ws and the H. It must also accurately reflect the headline, setting out what your audience will learn from reading the piece.

3. Structure the middle and conclusion

List all the main points covered in the introduction and decide which you are going to give the most weight to. Break each point into a section, starting with the most important first, and expand on each point using greater factual detail and quotes.

Add sidebars, images, infographics, videos, and advice and tips where appropriate. Include any relevant links to other topics, products or services on your website. End with a question that encourages further discussion or a call to action (eg to buy your product or service, or visit your website).

4. Edit and review thoroughly

After you have written your blog leave it for 24 hours and think about how you can improve it. Come back to it fresh the next day to add any new ideas and ensure it flows, makes sense and is factually correct.

Get a colleague or peer to review it to make sure you haven't missed anything.

Determine the best time to publish it, when the most people are likely to read it: typically that's at the start or end of the day, before and after they finish work.

5. Track your results

Seek feedback from your audience to learn what they did and didn't like about the blog. Run an analytics program such as Google Analytics to see where your traffic is coming from and how long they have spent reading it.

CASE STUDY

An IT consultancy client was struggling to drive business to its website. A review of the website told me it was putting customers off because it looked dated.

So we agreed to start a weekly blog on the website and an email newsletter campaign that was sent out to existing customers. We also plugged it on LinkedIn, where the client had a good following.

After a month, traffic to the website was up by 500%. The client also received 20 new leads as a direct result, while several of its existing customers chose to get back in touch.

SUMMARY

✓ The range of different online content formats is almost endless;

✓ You can use the same content, but present it slightly differently for each medium;

✓ The same basic rules for writing apply, though;

✓ Blogs are more conversational, while company reports and white papers are more formal;

✓ Remember to be consistent in your messaging across different formats

8

GETTING NOTICED
ON SOCIAL MEDIA

WHY SOCIAL MEDIA IS SO IMPORTANT

Social media has become the most popular way for people to get their news and share their views. Everyone is on there now, from the Queen, Beyoncé and Christiano Ronaldo to the man on the street.

More importantly, all of your customers and competitors are on social media, which means you need to be too. That enables you to see what they are doing, but also to maintain your own presence.

The younger generation being on social media whenever they're awake creates an excellent opportunity to promote your business to a wider audience. Because it is instant, news spreads much faster, so if you post content online, it has the potential to go viral within minutes or even seconds.

If your results from my five-step test were low, particularly in the area of social media, this chapter will enable you to develop a joined-up and successful strategy for your different platforms.

WHY YOU NEED TO BE ON LINKEDIN

With so many different social media platforms out there, how do you know which is the right one for you? I would say that if you are in business, there is only one you absolutely need to be on: LinkedIn.

LinkedIn is the best way to build up a network of business contacts and interact with them, whether that's promoting your product or service, finding new leads, staying in touch with customers, or keeping an eye on competitors. You can also join active discussion groups and follow key influencers, post, like, share and comment on content, as well as write and receive recommendations.

Think of it as your online CV that you use to sell yourself. Therefore you need to present yourself in the best possible light with relevant content targeted at your customers and suppliers.

HOW TO WRITE FOR LINKEDIN

Like every social media platform, LinkedIn is inundated with content. Someone posts a piece of content every second, so you need to make sure that you stand out from the crowd.

I find that publishing a **post** gets the most traction on LinkedIn. It is quite easy to do: all you need to do is copy and paste the link to your web page, blog or article that readers can click on and be taken to your website.

If you want to publish a more detailed piece, such as a white paper in its entirety, you should use an **article**. You can add headlines, sub-headings, main body text, images and captions to make it look like a professionally written piece. For example, see: **bit.ly/3x72KQX**.

To gauge your success, look at the comments and reactions underneath. You can also learn what your audience is more interested in by the number of views you receive at the bottom. You should also be looking to add value to the conversation by commenting on other people's posts and activity. You can do this, for example, by adding links to research you have done on that subject or sharing your insight and experience.

OTHER SOCIAL MEDIA

As I mentioned earlier, a host of different social media platforms exists. The main ones you need to know about are Facebook, Twitter, Instagram and Pinterest.

These are more picture-led, with fewer words, and lend themselves better to businesses that need to present their products visually. The golden rule when you are uploading content to social media is to make sure it is both relevant and timely, and is maintained regularly.

For more information about what social media platform may be right for you, get in touch at: **alexwrightcopywriter.com/contact**.

"

The golden rule when
you are uploading content
to social media is to make
sure it is both relevant
and timely, and
is maintained regularly.

"

CASE STUDY

An architect client was looking to get more business referrals. I suggested joining LinkedIn, where we set up a company page with its basic contact details.

From there, we built out the client's full profile and started to post a weekly blog discussing key issues customers experience with the design of their buildings. We also connected with peers and customers, signed up to relevant discussion groups and followed key influencers in the industry, as well as liking, sharing and commenting on others' posts.

Just by having a presence on LinkedIn, over time we were able to establish a strong network of contacts, some of who passed on leads that the client converted into sales. The client has now moved into posting video content to show what goes into the design process and the value customers will get from a professional job.

SUMMARY

✓ Social media is an excellent opportunity to promote your business to a wider audience;

✓ If you have a business you need to be on LinkedIn;

✓ LinkedIn is a great networking tool that enables you to find new leads, stay in touch with customers and peers, and keep an eye on competitors;

✓ Use posts and articles to engage your audience on LinkedIn

9

WHY YOU NEED THE MEDIA ON YOUR SIDE

WHY THE MEDIA ARE SO IMPORTANT

A lot of people are fearful of the media because of the effect their stories can have on their reputation. But they needn't be.

Speaking from experience, I have seen this from both sides, as a journalist, covering news stories about some of the world's leading businesses and CEOs, and as a copywriter, writing press release announcements. I can tell you that you actually stand to gain from using the media as a force for good. That is because journalists are always on the lookout for strong stories and if you have one, you can turn it to your advantage with some good free publicity for your business.

The more coverage you get in more publications, the more likely your customers are to read your story. That gives you greater credibility and keeps you in the front of their minds.

HOW TO HANDLE THE MEDIA

In order to use the media to your advantage, you have to know how to deal with them. The best way to do this is to build relationships with them, be as transparent as possible and regularly feed them good stories.

Here is my five-step plan to get and keep the media on your side:

1. Be proactive

In the same way that being up front pays dividends in the long run, being on the ball when it comes to marketing yourself can also be beneficial. Securing an editorial in a newspaper, magazine or online should be considered a free advertising hit.

If you have an interesting story to tell about yourself with a good angle, the media will lap it up. To decide whether your story is newsworthy, have a look for similar stories in the press. Your story idea may be specific to your company, but if you can put a national spin on it, you will make it more sellable. For example, say you are bucking the national trend with sales of your product at an all-time high despite a depressed economy, advertise that fact along with the secret to your success.

Write a press release of no more than 300 words outlining your key points, including a lively short quote from a senior figure. Add a punchy headline and your contact details, targeting journalists who may be genuinely interested in your story and who you have built up a good rapport with. For how to write the perfect press release visit **alexwrightcopywriter.com/blog-articles/ how-to-write-the-perfect-press-release**.

If it's really big news and you have the resources, call a press conference to make your announcement, where you can hand out the release. Also, putting out your story on the relevant social media channels makes it more likely to get picked up more quickly.

"

Make it easy for them by
providing the big story
they are looking for; they
will love you for it.

"

2. Tip them off

Journalists like nothing more than a press officer who tips them off about big stories. If you have a strong story to share, the media will soon become your best friend.

But it should not be a one-way street. You will reap the rewards further down the line if you happen to find yourself in a tricky situation, as they may be more inclined to treat it with sensitivity because you already have that relationship.

For example, I wrote several positive stories about a small car dealership. Then one day their showroom burned down overnight with many employees losing their jobs. But because I had developed that special relationship with them and they trusted me, I was the person they called to give the exclusive to.

3. Put yourself in their shoes

Imagine an agitated news editor breathing down your neck every five minutes, looking for an exclusive. As a journalist, of course you will go to any length to find the best lead.

But if you make it easy for them by providing the big story they are looking for; they will love you for it. It will also mean that you can feed them more positive stories in the future, which will have a greater chance of making it into print.

In this increasingly time-pressured environment, there is nothing more irritating for a journalist than a PR cold-calling, trying to pitch an uninspiring story that needs a lot of work. What journalists are looking for is clear and concise copy that gets straight to the point.

4. Be open and truthful

When you find yourself in a sticky situation, refusing to comment is often the worst thing you can do. It implies that you have done something wrong or have something to hide.

When journalists smell blood, they will stop at nothing to get their story, often at the cost of portraying you in a bad light. So be honest and up front about what has happened from the start.

If the allegations levelled at you are false, say so, providing proof of why they are false. If, on the other hand, you are in the wrong, you need to hold your hands up and admit it, because the more you try to hide something the more likely that the situation will get worse, or that something will come out later that compounds the problem.

If a reporter catches you off guard, say you need to check something and ask if you can call back. Then get your side of the story straight first. If, however, you are not in a position to comment at all, explain to them, calmly but firmly, why.

Before you say anything, however, consider how your comments are likely to be interpreted and used, how you will come across, and what the journalist's agenda is. Stick to your key message, don't say anything you might later regret and be prepared for any eventuality.

There are essentially two different ways the press can use your quotes: on or off the record. 'On the record' means they can use any comment you give them and attribute it to you, provided it is accurate.

'Off the record' means they cannot attribute the quote to you in their story. You should specify if you want your comments to be off the record before you say anything else, because most journalists will automatically assume it is on the record unless advised otherwise.

5. Invite them round

Journalism has changed greatly since the days of Fleet Street when scoops were obtained at the local pub. Now, increasingly, journalists have become desk-bound and rarely have the opportunity to go out and meet the man on the street.

By inviting the media into your business to meet you, with the promise of a good story at the end of it, you are offering valuable insight into how you operate. It will also help to reinforce the fact that you are open and transparent, and willing to co-operate when they need you.

If you want to learn more about dealing with the press, I provide media training. For further information get in touch at **alexwrightcopywriter.com/contact**.

CASE STUDY

A solicitor client was expanding its business and taking on more staff. I immediately identified it as a good news story, creating jobs for the town's economy, and pitched the story to the local newspapers.

We called a press conference at the firm's offices, inviting the local media and dignitaries, including the mayor, to announce the expansion. We issued press releases to the reporters. Then we arranged a photo shoot of the new team with the mayor afterwards.

The next day, the story ran with the picture on the front page of all the papers we had contacted and on their websites. The firm used the online version on its website. The positive feedback the firm received from existing customers was tremendous as the exposure served as a reminder that the firm was there to help. It also led to several enquiries from new customers who had read the article and wanted to use the firm's services.

SUMMARY

✓ Use the media to get good publicity;

✓ The more publications you appear in, the more likely you are to be noticed by customers;

✓ Build up a relationship with the media, be transparent and feed them good stories;

✓ Put yourself in their shoes and think about the angle they are looking for;

✓ Make it as easy as possible for them to get their story

10

HOW TO IMPROVE YOUR VERBAL COMMUNICATION

WHY THE SPOKEN WORD IS SO IMPORTANT

Just like the written word, the spoken word is an essential tool in your communication toolbox. Mastered properly, it can be used to tremendous effect to get your message across.

Whether you are the face of your business or prefer to be behind the scenes, you need to use strong verbal communication every day when dealing with customers or suppliers. Whenever you are talking with people, you are selling your business, so make sure you do it well.

Many of the same principles of writing apply to verbal communication. Speak clearly and concisely so that your audience understands what you are talking about.

HOW TO IMPROVE YOUR VERBAL SKILLS

There is a good chance that you will be asked to speak in public at some point in your career. That may be pitching a business idea or speaking on a panel.

Regardless of the occasion or your audience, here are my five golden rules:

1. **Stick to your allotted time limit.** If anything, speak for slightly less time and leave a few minutes at the end for questions. Do not talk for more than 20 minutes, which is an average person's maximum concentration span

2. **Know your subject inside out.** Think about the challenges your audience faces, how you can help them and the best way to get that information or advice across. Deliver your speech like a story, with a clear narrative that flows from beginning to end

3. **Smile and maintain a friendly disposition at all times.** Use humour where appropriate, but do not be too jokey

4. **Speak slowly, clearly and confidently with a purpose.** Writing a script with pauses for effect in the appropriate places will help you to maintain a good rhythm and pace

5. **Visit the venue where you are going to speak to gain familiarity with it.** Stand on the stage and practice delivering your speech to an empty room. Practice speaking in front of the mirror beforehand

Look at some of the greatest speakers in history (on YouTube, for example) and observe how they deliver their speeches. See what you can learn from them and incorporate it into your own style.

Before you start a speech, take a couple of deep breaths, drink a sip of water and compose yourself. Remember that even the most seasoned public speakers get nervous sometimes.

If you are speaking to one person, maintain eye contact with them at all times. If you are speaking to an audience from a lectern, stand tall and hold onto the sides to give a look of authority.

"

Make a maximum of
five main points; most
people can't remember
more than that.

"

Start by thanking the organiser for inviting you and your audience for attending. Use an ice-breaker to get them to warm to you.

Be yourself and address your audience directly. Speak slowly, loudly and clearly, emphasising the key points you want to make. Use your hands sparingly to reinforce your key messages and pause after each one to reflect.

Make each point succinctly, using anecdotes and real-life examples to expand upon them. Avoid using jargon and explain any acronyms you use.

Make a maximum of five main points; most people can't remember more than that. Try and break each point down into three parts; according to research, people are more receptive to facts that come in threes.

After five minutes, take a breath and have a sip or two. Look around the room to see if you are still engaging with your audience. If you are using a PowerPoint presentation, keep your slides to a minimum and avoid overloading them with too much information.

If you are on a panel, don't be afraid to challenge or disagree with a statement or point of view. But don't talk over or only argue with other panellists as this makes you look unprofessional.

At the end, recap all of your main points. Then open the floor to questions.

Above all, just try to relax and enjoy yourself. Set out to engage, entertain and inform your audience.

HOW TO SPEAK IN PERSON VS IN VIDEO CONFERENCE

Emails and letters serve a particular purpose, but there is no better way of communicating with someone than in person. You can get so much more out of them by talking face-to-face.

When speaking with someone in the same room, maintain eye contact at all times and don't cross your arms, slouch or fiddle. Use hand gestures where appropriate to illustrate key points, but don't overuse them.

Ask searching questions that are likely to elicit useful responses. Be firm but fair, saying only what you need to say, giving the other person an opportunity to talk and listen carefully. However, do not be afraid to challenge people if you disagree with what they say.

Many of the same principles of face-to-face meetings also apply to speaking on the phone. When arranging a call, do so well in advance, sending an email with the subjects you want to discuss.

Have a list of your main points prepared and handy to check as you go along. Stand up and smile at all times: your tone of voice will come across much better. Feel free to use hand gestures: nobody can see what you are doing at the other end of the phone.

Introduce yourself clearly and confidently, politely asking the other person how they are first. If it is going to be a long and detailed conversation, ask them whether they would mind if you record it.

An extension of the phone is the video conference. As a result of the pandemic, everyone is using it now. A host of communication tools are available that you can use including Zoom and Microsoft Teams.

Consider what will be in the picture, other than yourself. The background should be neither too busy, nor too interesting.

Make sure that random elements, such as children or animals, are not able to introduce themselves into the picture, distracting the participants.

Turn your camera and microphone on and talk as you would in person or on the phone. Be careful not to interrupt as you will quickly lose the flow of the conversation. Put yourself on mute, listen and wait until the other person has finished before responding to them.

Take advantage of all the tools at your disposal. You can also use these platforms to have a text conversation, brainstorm on a virtual whiteboard or carry out instant polls.

For more help with your verbal communication get in touch at **alexwrightcopywriter.com/contact**.

GETTING IN TOUCH
WITH YOUR SOFT SKILLS

In today's technologically advanced world, it seems that too many of us have lost the art of communication. Social media and text, while great inventions in their own right, have actually lowered our level of communication and made us lazier in the way we interact with others.

That is why it is essential to develop the right soft skills to be able to deal with people more effectively in the workplace. This is especially important if you are meeting clients every day, attending staff briefings or calling contractors working on site.

What are soft skills?

Soft skills are a combination of people, social and communication skills, character or personality traits, attitudes, career attributes, social intelligence and emotional intelligence that enables people to navigate their environment, work well with others, perform well and achieve their goals.

They include key skills such as common sense, the ability to deal with people and a positive, flexible attitude. When it comes to communication, soft skills are the tool you use to converse clearly and effectively with others, define and set expectations, and work collaboratively together with others on projects.

Fail to communicate your message properly or misunderstand what someone has said, and your whole project could collapse, potentially costing your company thousands or even millions of pounds. We communicate verbally and in writing every day, whether it's a face-to-face meeting or sending an email, so it's vital you use these five key soft skills:

1. **Listening:** to hear what someone is telling you

2. **Verbal:** to get your message across using words effectively

3. **Non-verbal:** using eye contact, body language, facial expressions and words

4. **Written:** to write powerfully and persuasively using the right tone of voice

5. **Presentation:** a combination of listening, verbal and written skills

How you use each of these skills is, however, markedly different, and depends on the situation you are in. Remember that your first contact with someone may be the only chance you get to impress them, so make it count.

In most cases you will want to be friendly, to open people up and get more out of them, but at other times you might need to be more direct and steer them away from going off at a tangent. You also want to be confident in your tone yet show respect and be empathetic to other people's causes, while keeping an open mind and listening to feedback.

Getting the right balance will enable you to more effectively greet someone, start a conversation, negotiate a deal, or sell your product or service. It can also help you to influence, delegate, appraise, motivate and manage teams.

Often, less is more: the more concise and to the point you are, the easier you are to understand and therefore the likelier you are to get more out of your conversation.

CASE STUDY

Accountants, by their nature, are often shy people. When an accountancy firm told me they had been asked to give a presentation to the local chamber of commerce about how to file a tax return digitally, I sensed their apprehension immediately.

Sitting down together, we came up with a structured plan for the content. Sticking to the guidelines we had been given, we were able to produce a compelling speech that would both engage and be of value to the audience.

After practicing it several times in front of me, my client felt confident enough to stand up in front of a room full of people and give his speech. It went down well and afterwards he was approached by several people who wanted to arrange a meeting to discuss their tax affairs.

SUMMARY

✓ Mastered properly, the spoken word can be just as powerful as the written word;

✓ Speak slowly, clearly and confidently;

✓ Be yourself and address your audience directly;

✓ Many of the same principles apply whether speaking in person or over the phone;

✓ There are many communications tools you can use such as Zoom and Microsoft Teams

WHAT NEXT?...

Having read this book, you now understand why you need a strong online presence and if you don't already have one, how to improve it, whether it is for your website, email newsletter or social media.

While you will be in a better position to move forward with your online content, you should also feel more confident in your writing ability and have a clear direction for what your content needs to achieve in order to start making more money and win customers.

As a little extra, here is my quick five-step checklist to help you focus on where you need to improve the online content on your website:

1. Do you understand what the wording on your website means?

2. Is it clear, concise and jargon-free?

3. Is it structured in a way that is easily accessible for your audience?

4. Does its tone of voice reflect your business?

5. Would it make you feel like buying your product or service?

To find out what you need to do next, take this free and simple five-step test: **alexwrightcopywriter.com/ website-and-online-content-review**.

If you need any further help with your online content or are interested to learn more about what you have read in this book, get in touch at **alexwrightcopywriter.com/ contact**. Don't feel like you are alone. I'd love to hear from you.

A quick favour...

Now you have read this book, let me know what you think about it by writing a short review on Amazon.

CONNECT WITH ALEX ONLINE AT:

ALEXWRIGHTCOPYWRITER.COM/CONTACT

UK.LINKEDIN.COM/IN/ALEX-WRIGHT-51887438

TWITTER.COM/ALEXWCOPYWRITER